Mary ENGELBREIT®

So Stitched CUTE!

W9-CNC-794

LEISURE ARTS, INC.
Little Rock, Arkansas

editorial staff

editor-in-chief	Susan White Sullivan
designer relations director	Debra Nettles
craft publications director	Cheryl Johnson
special projects director	Susan Frantz Wiles
senior prepress director	Mark Hawkins
art publications director	Rhonda Shelby
design team captain	Anne Stocks
design team	Kim Hamblin, Lori Wenger, and Becky Werle
technical writer	Lisa Lancaster
technical associates	Frances Huddleston, Mary Sullivan Hutcheson, and Jean Lewis
editorial writer	Susan McManus Johnson
art category manager	Lora Puls
graphic designer	Amy Temple
graphic artist	Becca Snider
production artist	Janie Marie Wright
imaging technicians	Brian Hall, Stephanie Johnson, and Mark R. Potter
photography manager	Katherine Laughlin
photostylist	Sondra Daniel
photographer	Ken West
publishing systems administrator	Becky Riddle
publishing systems assistant	Clint Hanson
mac information technology specialist	Robert Young

business staff

vice president and chief operations officer	Tom Siebenmorgen
director of finance and administration	Laticia Mull Dittrich
vice president, sales and marketing	Pam Stebbins
sales director	Martha Adams
marketing director	Margaret Reinold
creative services director	Jeff Curtis
information technology director	Hermine Linz
controller	Francis Caple
vice president, operations	Jim Dittrich
comptroller, operations	Rob Thieme
retail customer service manager	Stan Raynor
print production manager	Fred F. Pruss

Library of Congress Control Number: 2010923135
ISBN-13: 978-1-57486-393-2
ISBN-10: 1-57486-393-2

Stitched So Cute!

Discover the fun of embroidering whimsical gifts and accessories!

With a little fabric and easy embroidery, you can: Inspire the giggles of wee folk, fill your home with handmade décor, and thrill someone with a thoughtful gift. Many of these 53 Mary Engelbreit designs allow you to *choose how much embellishing* you want to do. You can simply embroider a playful design. You can also add color with markers or fusible appliqués. All of the reusable patterns are located in the handy envelope on the inside cover, so you'll always know where to find them. Enjoy the adventure of creating your own whimsical world with *Stitched So Cute*!

10

34

66

72

• general instructions • page 79

photo by Susan Jackson

mary engelbreit:
real life inspiration

In her childhood, Mary Engelbreit chose fantasy figures for her art subjects. It didn't take long, however, before she discovered the best source for creative inspiration.

"My art springs from real life," she says, "and real life just keeps happening."

Mary estimates that she has completed more than 5,000 illustrations in her career. She still dreams up every concept and draws every original illustration by hand. Mary and her staff go to great lengths to make certain that her artwork is reproduced as faithfully to her original work as possible.

Today, thousands of retailers nationally and internationally sell Mary Engelbreit products. It's an amazing degree of success for any company, but even more remarkable considering that it all began with a single-minded young girl who decided at age 11 that she was going to be an artist. And while Mary Engelbreit Studios has grown into a global licensing and retail business, that same girl still sits at its core, grown up now, but drawing her pictures with the same sense of wonder, imagination and enthusiasm.

one design—three ways

Feeling really artistic? Or just a little? That's the fun of these cute Mary Engelbreit designs—Mary provides the whimsical artwork, and you choose the way you want to embellish them!

Let's look at the owls from page 10 to see how the three techniques are done.

1 embroidery

This technique is the simplest of all. Just cover the lines of the transferred pattern with various embroidery stitches. You'll find helpful embroidery information on page 81.

Turn the page to see how the creative fun continues!

2 markers

If you loved coloring with markers when you were a kid, this technique may be the one for you. Simply outline the design and add desired details with embroidery stitches and then color it with markers. Notice all the subtle shading in the coloring. On page 83, we give you lots of tips on how to get just this look.

3 fabric appliqués

This technique will really appeal to the fabric lover. Make fusible fabric appliqués for each area of the design and then add details with felt, buttons, rickrack, and embroidery stitches. Turn to page 84 to find out more about fusible fabric appliqués.

All three methods are so much fun, it's okay if you have trouble picking just one. Why not try them all? You're going to love being your own creative artist. And just think of all the great gifts, children's items, and home accessories you'll make!

one design—three ways

wee folk

The youngest people in our lives are always open to the idea of **fun**—and that word perfectly describes these playful designs. Cute characters and images inspire Baby's imagination as they pose on wall décor, toys, and accessories. Older children will adore an apron or a set of storage bins to hold their toys. The clear instructions make it easy to complete these lighthearted, loveable creations.

nitey-nite owls

To create the artwork with fabric appliqués, follow these instructions. If you'd prefer to embroider or use markers, refer to the **General Instructions**, page 79, for information on transferring patterns, embroidery stitches, and using markers.

Finished Size: 18" x 12" (46 cm x 30 cm)

supplies

- 22" x 16" (56 cm x 41 cm) piece of white background fabric
- Two 18" (46 cm) wood stretcher strips
- Two 12" (30 cm) wood stretcher strips
- Fabric scraps for appliqués and large owl's body feathers and wings
- Paper-backed fusible web
- Embroidery floss
- 1¾ yds (1.6 m) of ⅝" (16 mm) wide grosgrain ribbon
- Scrap of gold felt
- Scrap of pink baby rickrack
- Staple gun
- Fabric glue
- Two ⁷⁄₁₆" (11 mm) diameter black two-hole buttons
- Four ¼" (7 mm) diameter black two-hole buttons
- Tracing paper or other thin paper
- Transfer supplies (see page 80)

instructions

Use pattern in envelope.

1 Follow **Transferring Patterns**, page 80, to transfer design to background fabric.

2 Follow **Making Fusible Fabric Appliqués**, page 84, to make appliqués for the following: branch; leaves; moon; large owl head, body (including head), eyes, and feet; medium owl body, wings, eyes, eye mask, tummy, and feet; small owl body, eyes, tummy, and feet.

3 For large owl wing pattern, trace wing and add ¼" seam allowances to all sides. Use pattern to cut 4 wings (2 in reverse).

4 Using transferred pattern for placement, fuse all appliqués except large owl head and eyes to background fabric.

5 Transfer detail lines to appliqués.

6 To make feathers on large owl body, cut 35 squares 2" x 2" from assorted scrap fabrics. Fold each square in half; fold in half again. Beginning at bottom of body and overlapping corners, position folded squares in a horizontal row across body. Sew row close to top edge. Continue to position and sew rows of squares to slightly above lower edge of head.

7 Fuse head appliqué over top edge of folded squares. Fuse eye appliqués to head.

8 Before sewing large owl wings, follow **Embroidery Stitches**, page 81, and use 3 strands of floss to work Lazy Daisy Stitches for feathers on each wing front. Matching right sides and raw edges and using a ¼" seam allowance, sew 1 wing and 1 wing in reverse together, leaving an opening for turning. Clip curves, turn right side out, and press. Sew opening closed. Repeat for remaining wing. Set wings aside.

9 Use 3 strands of floss to outline the design and add details. Work Stem Stitches around edges of each piece. On large owl, work Satin Stitches for eye details and French Knots around eyes. On small owl, work 3 Lazy Daisy Stitches for topknot and Blanket Stitches around eyes. Work Stem Stitches for veins on leaves.

10 Sew buttons to eyes. On large owl, tack wings to body along outer edge. On medium owl, glue rickrack to edge of wings.

11 Trace beak patterns onto tracing paper. Using the patterns, cut beaks from gold felt. Work two French Knots to attach each beak.

12 Following manufacturer's instructions, assemble stretcher strip frame. Centering design, stretch background fabric over edges of frame; staple fabric to back.

13 Glue grosgrain ribbon to the frame edges.

storybook friends

To create the wall art with markers, follow these instructions. If you'd prefer to embroider or make fabric appliqués, refer to the **General Instructions**, page 79, for information on transferring patterns, making fabric appliqués, and embroidery stitches.

Finished Size: 8" x 8" (20 cm x 20 cm) each

To make your project easier and more enjoyable, we encourage you to carefully read the General Instructions, page 79. Supplies and instructions are for making all 4 pieces.

supplies

- Four 12" x 12" (30 cm x 30 cm) pieces of white background fabric
- Prismacolor® Premier markers or permanent fabric markers
- Sixteen 8" (20 cm) wood stretcher strips
- Ribbon scraps
- Embroidery floss
- Staple gun
- Fabric glue
- Transfer supplies (see page 80)

instructions

Use patterns in envelope.

1 Follow **Transferring Patterns**, page 80, to transfer design to background fabric.

2 Follow **Embroidery Stitches**, page 81, and use 3 strands of floss to work Stem Stitches to outline design and add details. Work Satin Stitches on letters, eyes, highlights, Ducky's shirt, Puppy's nose and collar, scallops on Bunny's blouse, and Bunny's flower center. Work French Knots in Kitty's eyes, Puppy's nose, and Bunny's blouse and jumper. Work Running Stitches in Ducky's hat. Work Straight Stitches on Kitty's collar and for Ducky's beak and feathered edges.

3 Follow **Using Markers**, page 83, to color designs.

4 On bunny, glue ribbon to head.

5 Color border to edges of fabric.

6 Following manufacturer's instructions, assemble stretcher strip frame. Centering design, stretch background fabric over edges of frame; staple fabric to back.

my stuff stashers

To create the bins with fabric appliqués, follow these instructions. If you'd prefer to embroider or use markers, refer to the **General Instructions**, page 79, for information on transferring patterns, embroidery stitches, and using markers.

Finished Background Size: 6¼" x 6¼" (16 cm x 16 cm) each

To make your project easier and more enjoyable, we encourage you to carefully read the General Instructions, page 79. Supplies and instructions are for making 3 storage bins.

supplies

- Three canvas storage bins [Ours measure 10½"w x 10½"d x 11"h (27 cm x 27 cm x 28 cm)]
- Three 7¼" x 7¼" (18 cm x 18 cm) pieces of background fabric
- Fabric scraps for appliqués
- Paper-backed fusible web
- Embroidery floss
- Twelve ⅝" (16 mm) diameter white buttons
- Transfer supplies (see page 80)

instructions

Use patterns in envelope.

1 Follow **Transferring Patterns**, page 80, to transfer design to background fabric.

2 Follow **Making Fusible Fabric Appliqués**, page 84, to make appliqués. For piece behind car, make a 3⅝" x 3⅝" square appliqué.

3 Using transferred pattern for placement, fuse all appliqués to background fabric.

4 Transfer detail lines to appliqués.

5 Follow **Embroidery Stitches**, page 81, and use 3 strands of floss to work Stem Stitches around edges of each piece. On bear, work French Knots for eyes; work Stem Stitches for all other details. On car, work Stem Stitch motion lines and hubcaps; work a French Knot in each hubcap center.

6 To hem background fabric, press all edges ¼" to wrong side twice; stitch.

7 Sew through buttons and corners of fabric to attach the background fabric corners to each bin.

little artist's apron

To create the apron with markers, follow these instructions. If you'd prefer to embroider or make fabric appliqués, refer to the **General Instructions**, page 79, for information on transferring patterns, making fabric appliqués, and embroidery stitches.

*To make your project easier and more enjoyable, we encourage you to carefully read the **General Instructions**, page 79.*

supplies
- Purchased child's canvas apron
- Permanent fabric markers or Prismacolor® Premier markers
- Extra-wide double-fold bias tape
- 2³⁄₈ yds (2.2 m) of grosgrain ribbon
- Clear monofilament thread
- Embroidery floss
- Transfer supplies (see page 80)

instructions
Use patterns in envelope.

1 Carefully remove pocket and ties from apron; discard ties.

2 Follow **Transferring Patterns**, page 80, to transfer design to apron and pocket.

3 Follow **Embroidery Stitches**, page 81, and use 3 strands of floss to work Stem Stitches around the flowers, flower centers, leaves, paint palette, and for the words. Work a French Knot in the center of each small flower on bib and pocket.

4 Follow **Using Markers**, page 83, to color designs.

5 Measure across bib just below the flowers. Cut a bias tape length the determined measurement. Use clear thread to topstitch folded tape to bib.

6 Beginning on one side and mitering corners, sandwich pocket edges in bias tape; stitch in place. Topstitch pocket in place on apron. Mitering corners, sandwich apron edges in bias tape; stitch in place.

7 Cut two 18" lengths and two 24" lengths of ribbon. Fold 1 end of each ribbon length ½" to one side. Topstitch folded ends of 18" lengths to bib. Topstitch folded ends of 24" lengths to sides.

wee folk

17

naptime blankie

To create the blanket with embroidery, follow these instructions. If you'd prefer to make fabric appliqués or use markers, refer to the **General Instructions**, page 79, for information on transferring patterns, making fabric appliqués, and embroidery stitches. A plush blanket would not be suitable, so look for a blanket with a smooth finish.

*To make your project easier and more enjoyable, we encourage you to carefully read the **General Instructions**, page 79.*

supplies

- Purchased chenille baby blanket
- Size #5 pearl cotton thread
- Tissue paper
- Transfer supplies (see page 80)

instructions

Use pattern in envelope.

1 Trace pattern onto tissue paper.

2 Baste tissue paper to blanket along bottom edge.

3 Follow **Embroidery Stitches**, page 81, and use 1 strand of pearl cotton to work Stem Stitches to outline design and work French Knots for eyes through tissue paper and blanket.

4 When embroidery is complete, carefully tear away tissue paper.

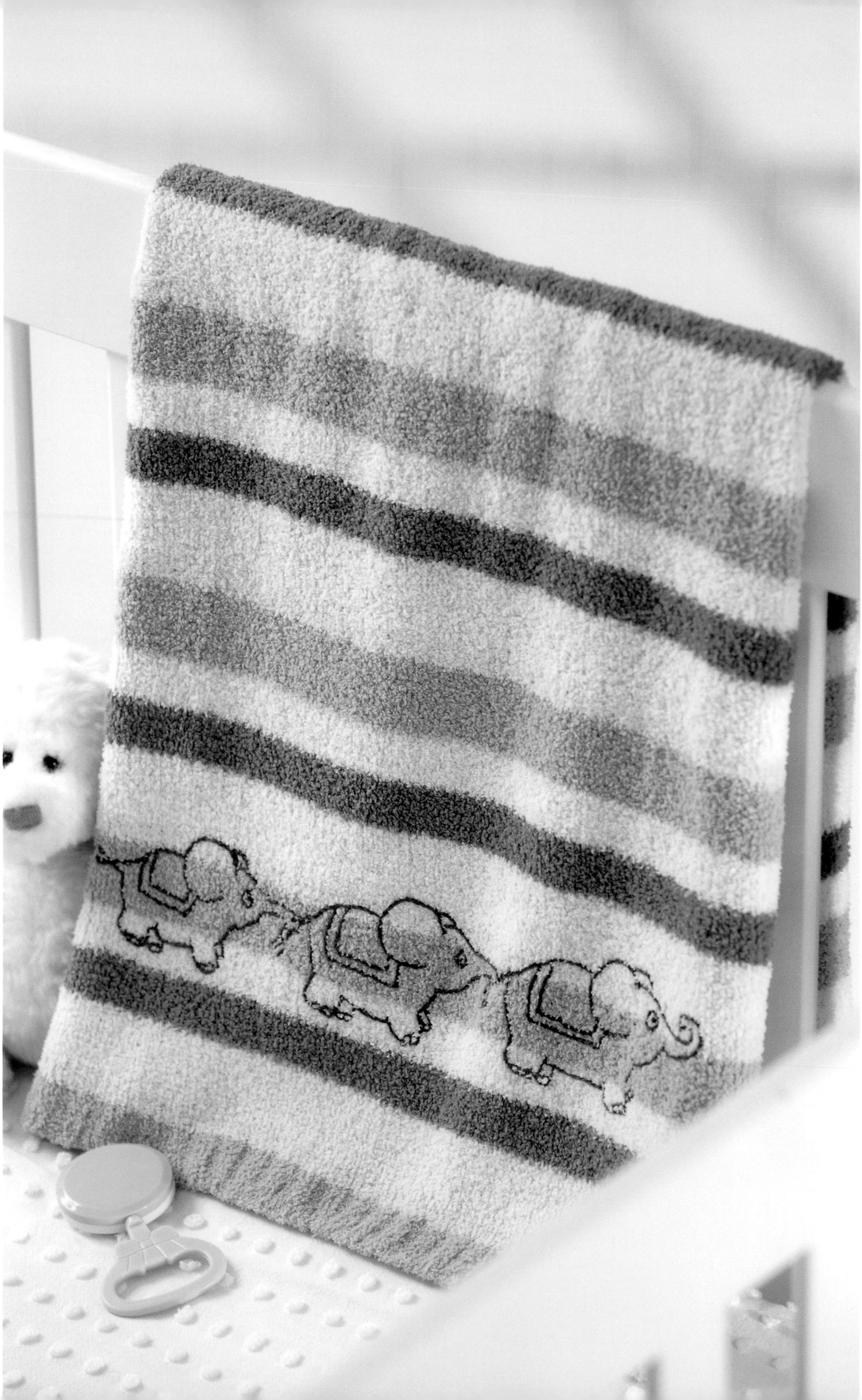

little lamb lovey

To create the lovey with appliqués, follow these instructions. If you'd prefer to embroider or use markers, refer to the **General Instructions**, page 79, for information on transferring patterns, embroidery stitches, and using markers.

Finished Size:
13½" x 13½" (34 cm x 34 cm)

To make your project easier and more enjoyable, we encourage you to carefully read the General Instructions, page 79.

supplies
- Two 13½" x 13½" (34 cm x 34 cm) pieces of white flannel fabric
- 2³⁄₈ yds (2.2 m) of 2" (51 mm) wide double-faced satin ribbon for binding and leaf appliqués
- 12" (30 cm) of ½" (13 mm) wide silk ribbon
- Paper-backed fusible web
- Ribbon scraps for appliqués
- Embroidery floss
- Clear monofilament thread
- Stabilizer
- Transfer supplies (page 80)

instructions
Use pattern in envelope.

1 Follow **Transferring Patterns**, page 80, to transfer design to 1 corner of 1 flannel piece.

2 Follow **Making Fusible Fabric Appliqués**, page 84, and use ribbon to make appliqués.

3 Using transferred pattern for placement, fuse all appliqués to flannel.

4 Transfer detail lines to appliqués.

5 Using clear thread, refer to **Appliqué**, page 86, to zigzag stitch around appliqué edges.

6 Follow **Embroidery Stitches**, page 81, and use 3 strands of floss to work Stem Stitches to outline and add details on the lamb and leaves. Work Satin Stitches for lamb's eyes.

7 For collar, sew a length of silk ribbon to neck. Tie a bow from remaining ribbon and tack in place.

Fig. 1

4"

8"

8 Matching wrong sides, layer flannel pieces; baste around edges.

9 For loop, make a 4" loop and tie a knot approximately 8" from one end of wide ribbon (**Fig. 1**).

10 Placing knot at one corner, fold remaining ribbon in half, sandwiching the flannel edges in between; pin in place, mitering corners and folding overlapping ribbon end to inside. Use clear thread to zigzag stitch ribbon in place, catching ribbon edges in stitching on front and back.

a fetching hoodie

To create the hoodie with fabric appliqués, follow these instructions. If you'd prefer to embroider or use markers, refer to the **General Instructions**, page 79, for information on transferring patterns, embroidery stitches, and using markers.

To make your project easier and more enjoyable, we encourage you to carefully read the General Instructions, page 79.

supplies
- Child's zip-front hoodie
- Fabric scraps for appliqués
- Paper-backed fusible web
- Embroidery floss
- 6" (15 cm) length of ³/₈" (10 mm) wide grosgrain ribbon
- Clear monofilament thread
- Stabilizer
- Transfer supplies (see page 80)

instructions
Use patterns in envelope.

1 Follow **Transferring Patterns**, page 80, to transfer design to hoodie.

2 Follow **Making Fusible Fabric Appliqués**, page 84, to make appliqués.

3 Using transferred pattern for placement, fuse all appliqués to hoodie.

4 Transfer detail lines to appliqués.

5 Refer to **Appliqué**, page 86, to zigzag stitch around appliqué edges using clear thread.

6 Follow **Embroidery Stitches**, page 81, and use 3 strands of floss to work Stem Stitches around edges of each piece. Work Satin Stitches for ears, nose, and tongue. Work Straight Stitches for eyebrows and bow detail lines. Work large French Knots for eyes.

7 Knot ribbon through zipper pull.

baby burpers

To create the burp pads with embroidery, follow these instructions. If you'd prefer to make fabric appliqués or use markers, refer to the **General Instructions**, page 79, for information on transferring patterns, making fabric appliqués, and embroidery stitches.

Finished Size:
7" x 16" (18 cm x 41 cm) each

*To make your project easier and more enjoyable, we encourage you to carefully read the **General Instructions**, page 79. Supplies and instructions are for making all burp pads.*

supplies

- Six 7" x 16" (18 cm x 41 cm) pieces of white flannel fabric
- Three 9½" x 18½" (24 cm x 47 cm) pieces of polka dot fabric
- Embroidery floss
- Transfer supplies (see page 80)

instructions

Use patterns in envelope.

1 Follow **Transferring Patterns**, page 80, to transfer design to 1 end of 1 flannel piece.

2 Follow **Embroidery Stitches**, page 81, and use 2 strands of floss to work Stem Stitches to outline and add details.

3 Center an unstitched flannel piece on wrong side of polka dot fabric; center stitched piece, stitched side up, on flannel piece. On one long edge, fold polka dot fabric to meet edge of flannel; fold again over flannel. Topstitch folded edge in place. Repeat for remaining long edge and each short edge.

too cute bibs!

To create the bibs with fabric appliqués, follow these instructions. If you'd prefer to embroider or use markers, refer to the **General Instructions**, page 79, for information on transferring patterns, embroidery stitches, and using markers.

To make your project easier and more enjoyable, we encourage you to carefully read the General Instructions, page 79. Supplies and instructions are for 3 bibs.

supplies
- Three 10" x 7" (25 cm x 18 cm) pieces of cream fabric
- Three 10" x 8" (25 cm x 20 cm) pieces of print fabric
- Three 10" x 13" (25 cm x 33 cm) pieces of flannel fabric for backing
- Fabric scraps for appliqués
- Paper-backed fusible web
- Embroidery floss
- Three 9" (23 cm) lengths of jumbo rickrack
- Three 48" (122 cm) lengths of extra-wide double-fold bias tape
- Six 12" (30 cm) lengths of 1" (25 mm) wide grosgrain ribbon
- Clear monofilament thread
- Tracing paper
- Stabilizer
- Transfer supplies (see page 80)

instructions
Use patterns in envelope.

1 Matching right sides and raw edges, sew long edge of cream fabric piece to print fabric piece using a ¼" seam allowance. Use clear thread to sew rickrack along seamline.

2 Aligning horizontal line on pattern with center of rickrack, use pattern to cut out bib. Use pattern to cut out backing. Set backing aside.

3 Follow **Transferring Patterns**, page 80, to transfer design to bib.

4 Follow **Making Fusible Fabric Appliqués**, page 84, to make appliqués.

5 Using transferred pattern for placement, fuse all appliqués to bib.

6 Transfer detail lines to appliqués.

7 Refer to **Appliqué**, page 86, to zigzag stitch around appliqué edges using clear thread.

8 Follow **Embroidery Stitches**, page 81, and use 6 strands of floss to work Satin Stitches for train wheel hubs and teapot highlights, flower center, and leaves. Work Stem Stitches or Backstitches around edges of each piece and for veins in leaves.

9 Matching wrong sides, baste bib front to bib backing.

10 Beginning near center back, sandwich the bib edges in 1 length of bias tape; stitch in place.

11 Fold under one end and sew 1 length of ribbon to wrong side at each neck edge.

georgie giraffe

supplies

- 11" x 22" (28 cm x 56 cm) piece of fabric for body, legs, and ears
- 4" x 4" (10 cm x 10 cm) piece of fabric for horns and hooves
- 2½ yds (2.3 m) **each** of 2 colors of yarn
- Embroidery floss
- Polyester fiberfill
- Tracing paper
- Transfer supplies (see page 80)

instructions

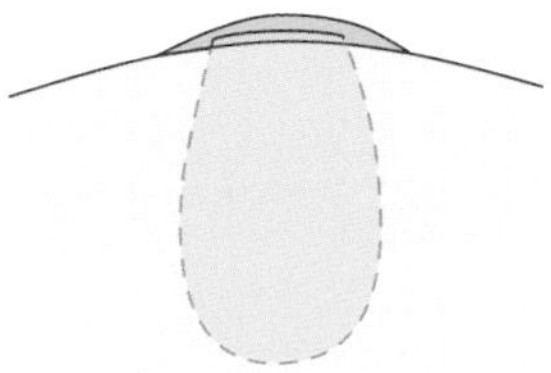

Use patterns in envelope. Match right sides and raw edges and use a ¼" seam allowance unless otherwise indicated.

1 Trace patterns (including symbols) onto tracing paper; cut out.

2 Pin tracing paper pattern to fabrics. Cut out fabric pieces as directed on patterns. Refer to **Transferring Patterns**, page 80, to transfer symbols to **wrong** side of pieces. Transfer eye, nose, and mouth details to **right** side of pieces.

3 Follow **Embroidery Stitches**, page 81, and use 3 strands of floss to work Satin Stitch for eyes. Work a small Cross Stitch in center of each eye. Work Stem Stitches for nose and mouth details.

4 To make ears, sew 1 ear and 1 ear in reverse together. Turn ear right side out and press. Topstitch along the curved edge. Repeat to make a total of 2 ears.

5 To attach ear, cut a small slit in body piece as indicated on pattern. Fold body piece right sides together at slit. From right side, slip 1 ear through slit. aligning raw edges of ear and raw edges of slit (**Fig. 1**). Securely catching all edges, sew as close to cut edges as possible. Repeat for remaining ear.

6 To make horns, sew 1 horn and 1 horn in reverse together. Turn horn right side out and press. Stuff horn firmly with fiberfill. Repeat for remaining horn. Hand sew horns to head.

Fig. 1

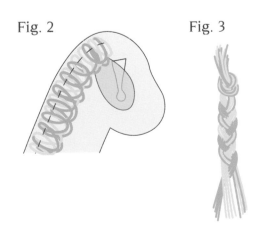

Fig. 2

Fig. 3

7 Mane will be attached to right side of 1 body piece along neck edge. Alternating each yarn color and forming consistent size loops, baste yarn between ✳ symbols, using a ⅛" seam allowance (**Fig. 2**).

8 For tail, cut a total of twelve 12" strands of assorted yarns. Align the yarn lengths and tie a knot near 1 end. Tape knot to flat surface. Divide yarn lengths into 3 groups of 4 strands each. Braid groups together for approximately 2" (**Fig. 3**). Tie a length of yarn around end of braid to secure. Trim yarn ends as desired. Baste tail at ◆ symbol, using a ⅛" seam allowance.

9 Leaving an opening between ●'s, sew bodies together. Clip curves and turn right side out. Stuff firmly with fiberfill and hand sew opening closed.

Instructions continued on page 32.

my best-dressed pals

To create the framed pieces with fabric appliqués, follow these instructions. If you'd prefer to embroider or use markers, refer to the **General Instructions**, page 79, for information on transferring patterns, embroidery stitches, and using markers.

Finished Size: 11" x 14" (28 cm x 36 cm) each

To make your project easier and more enjoyable, we encourage you to carefully read the General Instructions, page 79. Supplies and instructions are for making all framed pieces.

supplies

- Three 15" x 18" (38 cm x 46 cm) pieces of background fabric
- Fabric scraps for appliqués
- Embroidery floss
- Paper-backed fusible web
- Assorted trims (We used ribbons and buttons.)
- Three 11" x 14" (28 cm x 36 cm) picture frames
- Three 11" x 14" (28 cm x 36 cm) pieces of lightweight batting
- Three 11" x 14" (28 cm x 36 cm) pieces of lightweight cardboard
- Masking tape
- Transfer supplies (see page 80)

instructions

Use patterns in envelope. If you are using a striped or patterned background, as we did, we recommend fusing lightweight fusible interfacing to the wrong side of all appliqué fabrics before cutting appliqués to prevent background showing through appliqués.

1 Follow **Transferring Patterns**, page 80, to transfer design to background fabric.

2 Follow **Making Fusible Fabric Appliqués**, page 84, to make appliqués.

3 Using transferred pattern for placement, fuse all appliqués to background fabric.

4 Transfer detail lines to appliqués.

Instructions continued on page 32.

my best-dressed pals
continued from page 31

continued from page 31

5 Follow **Embroidery Stitches**, page 81, and use 3 strands of floss to work Stem Stitches around edges of each piece and for detail lines. Work Satin Stitches for eyes, birds' beaks, bear's nose, and chick's beak and highlights. Work French Knots for birds' eyes. Work Chain Stitch for elephant's tail.

6 For bear's fluffy pom-poms and elephant's tail, tack fifteen to twenty 2" floss lengths to the background. Clip and fluff the ends.

7 Sew buttons to chick and elephant for flower centers and to elephant's pants. Glue ribbons to elephant for suspenders.

8 Place batting on cardboard. Center and stretch design over batting; tape fabric to back of cardboard. Insert cardboard into frame and tape in place.

georgie giraffe
continued from page 29

continued from page 29

10 Leaving short straight edges open and an opening between ●'s, sew 1 leg and 1 leg in reverse together from ★ to ★. Matching ★'s, sew hoof to leg. Repeat to make a total of 4 legs.

11 Turn legs right side out and stuff firmly with fiberfill. Hand sew opening closed.

12 Securely hand sew legs to body.

13 Follow **Embroidery Stitches**, page 81, and use 2 strands of floss to work Blanket Stitches on each side of body seam. Work Blanket Stitches along leg seams.

home cute home

Why make your home a castle when it can be a cozy cottage, instead? These softly stitched house warmers are wonderful gifts for new homeowners. In fact, anyone who loves to spend time in their haven will adore the fresh linens, plump pillows, and other unique decorative items in this collection. From pet bins to a pretty table topper, each pattern is enhanced with playful Mary Engelbreit designs.

embroidered pillowcase

*To make your project easier and more enjoyable, we encourage you to carefully read the **General Instructions**, page 79.*

supplies

- Pillowcase
- Embroidery floss
- Clear monofilament thread
- 1¼ yds (1.1 m) of jumbo rickrack
- Transfer supplies (see page 80)

instructions

Use pattern in envelope.

1 Follow **Transferring Patterns**, page 80, to transfer design to a pillowcase corner.

2 Follow **Embroidery Stitches**, page 81, and use 3 strands of floss to work Stem Stitches over design lines and 4 strands to work French Knot sunrays.

3 Overlapping ends at back, use clear thread to zigzag stitch rickrack to pillowcase.

marker pillowcase

*To make your project easier and more enjoyable, we encourage you to carefully read the **General Instructions**, page 79.*

supplies

- Pillowcase
- Embroidery floss
- Permanent fabric markers or Prismacolor® Premier markers
- Clear monofilament thread
- 1¼ yds (1.1 m) of ribbon
- Transfer supplies (see page 80)

instructions

Use pattern in envelope.

1 Follow **Transferring Patterns**, page 80, to transfer design to pillowcase corner.

2 Follow **Embroidery Stitches**, page 81, and use 3 strands of floss to work Stem Stitches over all design lines and 4 strands to work French Knot sunrays.

3 Follow **Using Markers**, page 83, to color design.

4 Overlapping ends at back, use clear thread to sew ribbon to pillowcase.

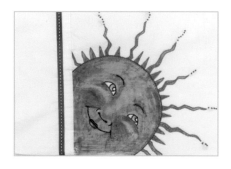

Instructions for appliqued pillowcase and sheet found on pages 36 & 37.

COUNT YOUR BLESSINGS

fabric appliqué pillowcase

To make your project easier and more enjoyable, we encourage you to carefully read the General Instructions, page 79.

supplies

- Pillowcase
- 12" x 12" (30 cm x 30 cm) fabric piece for sun appliqué
- Felt scrap for circles
- 1/2" (13 mm) dia. hole punch
- Paper-backed fusible web
- Stabilizer
- Clear monofilament thread
- Embroidery floss
- 1 1/4 yds (1.1 m) **each** of 2 grosgrain ribbons
- Transfer supplies (see page 80)

instructions

Use pattern in envelope.

1 Follow **Transferring Patterns**, page 80, to transfer design to a pillowcase corner, repeating vine around entire pillowcase.

2 Follow **Making Fusible Fabric Appliqués**, page 84, to make appliqué. Punch desired number of felt circles.

3 Using transferred pattern for placement, fuse appliqué to pillowcase.

4 Transfer detail lines to appliqué.

5 Follow **Appliqué**, page 86, to zigzag stitch around appliqué edges using clear thread.

6 Follow **Embroidery Stitches**, page 81, and use 2 strands of floss to work Stem Stitches around edges of appliqué and along detail lines and vine. Use 3 strands of floss to work Satin Stitches for eyes and cheek highlights and to work Lazy Daisy Stitches for leaves on vine. Use 4 strands of floss to work French Knot sunrays.

7 Overlapping ends at back, use clear thread to sew ribbons to pillowcase. Use 3 strands of floss and a French Knot to attach each felt circle. Work French Knots between felt circles for an additional touch.

home cute home

fabric appliqué sheet

To make your project easier and more enjoyable, we encourage you to carefully read the **General Instructions***, page 79.*

supplies

- Flat sheet
- Fabric scraps for sun, bird, and letter appliqués
- Felt scrap for circles
- $1/2$" (13 mm) dia. hole punch
- Paper-backed fusible web
- Stabilizer
- Clear monofilament thread
- Embroidery floss
- Ribbons
- Transfer supplies (see page 80)

instructions

Use pattern in envelope.

1 Follow **Transferring Patterns**, page 80, to transfer design to sheet hem placing design so that it can be read when sheet is turned back and repeating vine across sheet.

2 Follow **Making Fusible Fabric Appliqués**, page 84, to make sun and letter appliqués. Punch desired number of felt circles.

3 Folding ribbon ends under at each sheet edge, use clear thread to sew ribbons to sheet. Use 3 strands of floss and a French Knot to attach each felt circle. Work French Knots between felt circles for a colorful accent.

4 Using transferred pattern for placement, fuse appliqués to sheet.

5 Refer to **Appliqué**, page 86, to zigzag stitch around appliqué edges using clear thread.

6 Transfer detail lines to appliqués.

7 Follow **Embroidery Stitches**, page 81, and use 3 strands of floss to work Stem Stitches around edges of appliqués and along detail lines and vine. Use 3 strands of floss to work Satin Stitches for bird's beak and feet and to work Lazy Daisy Stitches for leaves on vine. Use 1 floss strand to work Stem Stitches for sun's facial details.

a bevy of blooms

To create the banner with fabric appliqués, follow these instructions. If you'd prefer to embroider or use markers, refer to the **General Instructions**, page 79, for information on transferring patterns, embroidery stitches, and using markers.

Finished Size: 22½" x 40" (57 cm x 102 cm) including fringe

To make your project easier and more enjoyable, we encourage you to carefully read General Instructions, page 79.

supplies
- 23½" x 40½" (60 cm x 103 cm) piece of fabric for banner front (Ours is linen.)
- 23½" x 40½" (60 cm x 103 cm) piece of fabric for backing
- Assorted scraps of batik cotton fabrics for flower and center appliqués
- Assorted scraps of batik and print cotton fabrics for leaf appliqués
- 6 yds (5.5 m) of 1" (25 mm) wide dark green grosgrain ribbon
- 4 yds (3.7 m) of 1" (25 mm) wide light green grosgrain ribbon
- 1⅜ yds (1.3 m) of ⅜" (10 mm) wide trim
- Embroidery floss
- Clear monofilament thread
- Paper-backed fusible web
- Stabilizer
- Transfer supplies (see page 80)

instructions
Use patterns in envelope. Use a ½" seam allowance throughout.

1 Follow **Transferring Patterns**, page 80, to transfer design to banner front.

2 Follow **Making Fusible Fabric Appliqués**, page 84, to make appliqués.

3 Using transferred pattern for placement, fuse all appliqués to banner front.

Instructions continued on page 54.

blooms for the table

fabric appliqué table topper

Finished Size: 23" x 23" (58 cm x 58 cm)

To make your project easier and more enjoyable, we encourage you to carefully read General Instructions, page 79.

supplies

- 23" x 23" (58 cm x 58 cm) piece of blue wool felt for background
- 18" x 18" (46 cm x 46 cm) cream cloth napkin
- Scraps of blue and olive wool felt
- Clear monofilament thread
- Embroidery floss
- Stabilizer
- Twelve ½" (13 mm) dia. navy buttons
- 2⅝ yds (2.4 m) of olive jumbo rickrack
- Fabric glue
- Transfer supplies (see page 80)

instructions

Use patterns in envelope.

1 Follow **Transferring Patterns**, page 80, to transfer design to napkin corners.

2 Use patterns to cut 4 leaf clusters and 12 flowers from felt.

3 Using transferred pattern for placement, pin felt pieces to napkin.

4 Refer to **Appliqué**, page 86, to zigzag stitch around edges of all felt pieces using clear thread.

5 Follow **Embroidery Stitches**, page 81, and use 3 strands of floss to work Blanket Stitches around felt pieces. Work Stem Stitch leaves, flower stems, and leaf details. Sew buttons to flowers.

6 Round corners of blue background (use a small plate as a guide). Use 2 strands of floss to work Running Stitches to attach napkin to center of background. Glue rickrack to background.

Matching Place Mat and Embroidered Napkin instructions found on page 55.

So MUCH OF WHAT WE KNOW OF LOVE WE LEARN AT HOME.

"love-ly" rose pillows

To create the pillow with markers, follow these instructions. If you'd prefer to embroider or make fabric appliqués, refer to the **General Instructions**, page 79, for information on transferring patterns, making fabric appliqués, and embroidery stitches.

love at home pillow

Finished Size: 18" x 18" (46 cm x 46 cm)

To make your project easier and more enjoyable, we encourage you to carefully read General Instructions, page 79.

supplies
- 11" x 19" (28 cm x 48 cm) piece of cream fabric
- 5" x 19" (13 cm x 48 cm) piece each of 2 print fabrics
- 19" x 19" (48 cm x 48 cm) piece of fabric for pillow back
- ¹/₂ yd (46 cm) of fabric for welting
- 2¹/₈ yds (1.9 m) of ¹/₂" (13 mm) dia. cord
- Prismacolor® Premier markers or permanent fabric markers
- Embroidery floss
- 18" x 18" (46 cm x 46 cm) pillow form
- Transfer supplies (see page 80)

instructions
Use patterns in envelope. Match right sides and raw edges and use a ¹/₂" seam allowance throughout.

1 Follow **Transferring Patterns**, page 80, to transfer design to cream fabric.

2 Follow **Embroidery Stitches**, page 81, and use 3 strands of floss to work Stem Stitches over all design lines.

3 Follow **Using Markers**, page 83, to color design.

4 Sew 1 print fabric piece to each side of cream fabric piece.

5 Refer to **Adding Welting**, page 87, to finish pillow.

Instructions for Floral Pillow on page 56.

big, beautiful blooms!

Finished Size: 16" x 20"
(41 cm x 51 cm)

supplies

- 21" x 25" (53 cm x 64 cm) piece of black wool felt for background
- 13" x 22" (33 cm x 56 cm) piece of rose wool felt for outer petals
- 8" x 15" (20 cm x 38 cm) piece of light rose wool felt for inner petals
- 6" x 20" (15 cm x 51 cm) piece of olive wool felt for leaves
- 6" x 20" (15 cm x 51 cm) piece of green overdyed felted wool for leaves
- Scrap of light yellow wool felt for flower centers
- Clear monofilament thread
- Stabilizer
- Embroidery floss
- Polyester fiberfill
- 16" x 20" (41 cm x 51 cm) artist canvas or ready-made frame
- Transfer supplies (see page 80)

instructions

Use patterns in envelope.

1. Use patterns to cut 8 outer petals, 8 inner petals, 8 centers, 9 leaf A's (5 in reverse) and 10 leaf B's (3 in reverse).
2. Arrange and pin flower and leaf pieces on background felt.

For a more traditional look, insert canvas into a frame.

3 Refer to **Appliqué**, page 86, to zigzag stitch around some appliqué edges using clear thread. Leaving some edges unstitched creates a wonderful dimensional effect.

4 Follow **Embroidery Stitches**, page 81, and use 6 strands of floss to work Chain Stitches around and on appliqués as desired. Lightly stuff each flower center before working a French Knot to close.

5 Wrap background felt around artist canvas and staple to wood on back.

hot stuff

To create the hot pads with fabric appliqués, follow these instructions. If you'd prefer to embroider or use markers, refer to the **General Instructions**, page 79, for information on transferring patterns, embroidery stitches, and using markers.

Finished Size: 6¹/₂" x 8¹/₂" (17 cm x 22 cm) each

*To make your project easier and more enjoyable, we encourage you to carefully read **General Instructions**, page 79. Supplies and instructions are for making 2 hot pads.*

supplies

- Four 6¹/₂" x 8¹/₂" (17 cm x 22 cm) pieces of fabric for background and backing
- ¹/₄ yd (23 cm) of fabric for binding
- Fabric scraps for appliqués
- Two 6¹/₂" x 8¹/₂" (17 cm x 22 cm) pieces of batting
- Paper-backed fusible web
- Stabilizer
- Clear monofilament thread
- Embroidery floss
- Transfer supplies (see page 80)

instructions

Use pattern in envelope.

1 Follow **Transferring Patterns**, page 80, to transfer design to background fabric.

2 Follow **Making Fusible Fabric Appliqués**, page 84, to make appliqués.

3 Using transferred pattern for placement, fuse all appliqués to background fabric.

4 Transfer detail lines to appliqués.

5 Follow **Embroidery Stitches**, page 81, and use 3 strands of floss to work Stem Stitches around edges of all appliqués. Work Satin Stitches for cherry highlights.

6 Layer backing (wrong side up), batting, and appliquéd background (right side up); baste together along outer edges.

7 Cut a 3" x 40" strip of binding fabric. Press one long edge ³/₄" to wrong side. Using a ³/₄" seam allowance, sew unpressed long edge to front of layered hot pad along outer edges, mitering corners. Fold binding to back and whipstitch the pressed edge to backing, covering raw fabric edges.

8 For hanger, sew a 6" twill tape length to hot pad back.

two for tea

To create the tea towels with embroidery, follow these instructions. If you'd prefer to make fabric appliqués or use markers, refer to the **General Instructions**, page 79, for information on transferring patterns, making fabric appliqués, and embroidery stitches.

Design Size: approx. 4" x 2³/₈" (10 cm x 6 cm)

*To make your project easier and more enjoyable, we encourage you to carefully read the **General Instructions**, page 79. Supplies and instructions are for making 2 tea towels.*

supplies
- Two tea towels [ours measure 15¹/₂" x 27" (39 cm x 69 cm)]
- Embroidery floss
- Jumbo rickrack
- Ball fringe trim
- Transfer supplies (see page 80)

instructions
Use patterns in envelope.

1 Follow **Transferring Patterns**, page 80, to transfer designs to tea towels.

2 Follow **Embroidery Stitches**, page 81, and use 3 strands of floss to work Stem Stitches over all design lines. Work French Knots for eyes.

3 Turning under raw ends, sew rickrack and ball fringe to towel.

bins for furry friends

To create the bins with markers, follow these instructions. If you'd prefer to embroider or make fabric appliqués, refer to the **General Instructions**, page 79, for information on transferring patterns, making fabric appliqués, and embroidery stitches.

Design Size: approx. 4" x 5³/₄" (10 cm x 15 cm)

*To make your project easier and more enjoyable, we encourage you to carefully read the **General Instructions**, page 79. Supplies and instructions are for 2 bins.*

supplies

- Two canvas storage bins [ours measure 13"w x 10"d x 7¹/₂"h (33 cm x 25 cm x 19 cm)]
- Embroidery floss
- Prismacolor® Premier markers or permanent fabric markers
- Jumbo rickrack
- Fabric glue
- Transfer supplies (see page 80)

instructions

Use patterns in envelope.

1 Follow **Transferring Patterns**, page 80, to transfer designs to bins.

2 Follow **Embroidery Stitches**, page 81, to work Stem Stitches over all design lines.

3 Follow **Using Markers**, page 83, to color designs.

4 Glue rickrack to storage bins, overlapping ends at bin back.

birds of a feather pillow

To create the pillow with markers, follow these instructions. If you'd prefer to embroider or make fabric appliqués, refer to the **General Instructions**, page 79, for information on transferring patterns, making fabric appliqués, and embroidery stitches.

Finished Size: 16" x 16" (41 cm x 41 cm)

To make your project easier and more enjoyable, we encourage you to carefully read General Instructions, page 79.

supplies
- 17" x 17" (43 cm x 43 cm) piece of gold fabric
- 17" x 17" (43 cm x 43 cm) piece of fabric for back
- Prismacolor® Premier markers or permanent fabric markers
- Embroidery floss
- 2⅛ yds (1.9 m) of jumbo rickrack
- 16" x 16" (41 cm x 41 cm) pillow form
- Transfer supplies (see page 80)

instructions
Use pattern in envelope.

1 Follow **Transferring Patterns**, page 80, to transfer design to gold fabric.

2 Follow **Embroidery Stitches**, page 81, and use 3 strands of floss to work Stem Stitches over all design lines and to work French Knots for eyes.

3 Follow **Using Markers**, page 83, to color design.

4 Using a ½" seam allowance, center and baste rickrack to pillow front along seamline. Leaving an opening for turning, sew back to front. Turn right side out, insert pillow form, and sew opening closed.

a bevy of blooms
continued from page 38

4 Transfer detail lines to appliqués.

5 Refer to **Appliqué**, page 86, to zigzag stitch around appliqué edges using clear thread.

6 Follow **Embroidery Stitches**, page 81, and use 3 strands of floss to work Stem Stitches around edges of each appliqué. Randomly work Satin Stitch highlights on flowers and flower centers.

7 Matching right sides and raw edges, sew front to backing along sides and bottom. Turn right side out and press.

8 Cut two 40" lengths from each green ribbon. Pin dark green ribbon along each side edge of banner front. Pin light green ribbon beside dark green ribbon. Zigzag stitch along ribbon edges and along center where ribbons meet.

9 Cut trim in half. Turn top of banner 3" to wrong side; pin. Pin 1 length of trim 2" from fold. Zigzag stitch trim to banner, creating a rod pocket.

10 Cut remaining dark green ribbon in 8" lengths. Fold each length in half; press. Cut remaining light green ribbon in 4" lengths. Alternating colors and spacing evenly, pin ribbons to lower edge of banner. Pin remaining length of trim over ribbons and zigzag stitch in place.

home cute home

marker place mat

continued from page 40

Finished Size: 19" x 14¼"
(48 cm x 36 cm)

*To make your project easier and more enjoyable, we encourage you to carefully read **General Instructions**, page 79. Supplies and instructions are for making 1 place mat.*

supplies

- 19" x 14¼" (48 cm x 36 cm) cream place mat
- Permanent fabric markers or Prismacolor® Premier markers
- Embroidery floss
- Three ½" (13 mm) dia. buttons
- Transfer supplies (see page 80)

instructions

Use patterns in envelope.

1 Follow **Transferring Patterns**, page 80, to transfer design to 1 place mat corner.

2 Follow **Embroidery Stitches**, page 81, and use 3 strands of floss to work Stem Stitches over all design lines.

3 Follow **Using Markers**, page 83, to color design.

4 Sew buttons to flowers.

embroidered napkin

continued from page 40

Finished Size: 18" x 18"
(46 cm x 46 cm)

*To make your project easier and more enjoyable, we encourage you to carefully read **General Instructions**, page 79. Supplies and instructions are for making 1 napkin.*

supplies

- 18" x 18" (46 cm x 46 cm) cream napkin
- Embroidery floss
- Transfer supplies (see page 80)

instructions

Use patterns in envelope.

1 Follow **Transferring Patterns**, page 80, to transfer design to 1 napkin corner.

2 Follow **Embroidery Stitches**, page 81, and use 2 strands of floss to work Stem Stitches over all design lines. Add French Knot highlights to flowers.

3 Use 2 strands of floss to work Running Stitches near napkin edges.

To create the pillow with fabric appliqués, follow these instructions. If you'd prefer to embroider or use markers, refer to the **General Instructions**, page 79, for information on transferring patterns, embroidery stitches, and using markers.

floral pillow
Continued from page 43

*To make your project easier and more enjoyable, we encourage you to carefully read **General Instructions**, page 79.*

Finished Size: 14" x 14" (36 cm x 36 cm)

supplies

- 15" x 15" (38 cm x 38 cm) piece of print fabric for background
- 15" x 15" (38 cm x 38 cm) piece of print fabric for pillow back
- Scraps of 3 print fabrics for appliqués
- 1³/₄ yds (1.6 m) of jumbo rickrack
- Paper-backed fusible web
- Clear monofilament thread
- Embroidery floss
- Stabilizer
- 14" x 14" (36 cm x 36 cm) pillow form
- Transfer supplies (see page 80)

instructions

Use patterns in envelope. Match right sides and raw edges and use a ¹/₂" seam allowance throughout.

1 Follow **Transferring Patterns**, page 80, to transfer design to background fabric.

2 Follow **Making Fusible Fabric Appliqués**, page 84, to make appliqués.

3 Using transferred pattern for placement, fuse appliqués to background fabric.

4 Refer to **Appliqué**, page 86, to zigzag stitch around appliqué edges.

5 Follow **Embroidery Stitches**, page 81, and use 3 strands of floss to work Stem Stitches around edges of appliqués.

6 Using a ¹/₂" seam allowance, center and baste rickrack to pillow front along seamline. Leaving an opening for turning, sew back to front. Turn right side out, insert pillow form, and sew opening closed.

from me to you

Few joys exceed that of giving someone a handmade item—unless it's receiving such a special gift! Take time to "Breit-en" the lives of family and friends with these pretty and practical accessories. Create fresh ideas for the kitchen with a bread cloth or apron. Treat a stitcher to a pair of woodsy pincushions and a handy sewing kit. To present your heartwarming gift, make a flower-tied pouch or one of several sweet tags!

fresh bread!

To create the bread cloth with markers, follow these instructions. If you'd prefer to embroider or make fabric appliqués, refer to the **General Instructions**, page 79, for information on transferring patterns, making fabric appliqués, and embroidery stitches.

*To make your project easier and more enjoyable, we encourage you to carefully read the **General Instructions**, page 79.*

Finished Size: 20" x 20" (51 cm x 51 cm)

supplies
- 20" x 20" (51 cm x 51 cm) square of light-colored fabric
- ³⁄₈ yd (34 cm) of fabric for binding
- Permanent fabric markers or Prismacolor® Premier markers
- Embroidery floss
- Transfer supplies (see page 80)

instructions
Use pattern in envelope.

1 Follow **Transferring Patterns**, page 80, to transfer design to a corner of fabric square.

2 Follow **Embroidery Stitches**, page 81, and use 2 strands of floss to work Stem Stitches over all lines.

3 Follow **Using Markers**, page 83, to color design.

4 Cut three 4" x 40" strips of binding fabric. For binding, sew strips together end to end.

5 Press binding in half lengthwise; unfold. Press each long edge to wrong side to meet pressed line.

6 Sandwich and pin binding to bread cloth, mitering corners. Topstitch in place.

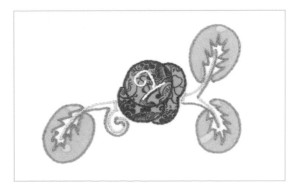

Fabric Appliqué

Embroidery

miss baker's apron

To create the apron with fabric appliqués, follow these instructions. If you'd prefer to embroider or use markers, refer to the **General Instructions**, page 79, for information on transferring patterns, embroidery stitches, and using markers.

To make your project easier and more enjoyable, we encourage you to carefully read the **General Instructions,** *page 79.*

supplies

- 25¹/₂" x 18¹/₂" (65 cm x 47 cm) piece of print fabric
- 19" x 24" (48 cm x 61 cm) piece of solid-colored fabric
- Fabric scraps for appliqués
- Paper-backed fusible web
- Embroidery floss
- 19" (48 cm) of jumbo rickrack
- 1⁵/₈ yds (1.5 m) of 1" (25 mm) wide grosgrain ribbon
- ¹/₄" (7 mm) button
- Clear monofilament thread
- Stabilizer
- Transfer supplies (see page 80)

instructions

Use pattern in envelope. Match right sides and raw edges and use a ¹/₄" seam allowance throughout.

1 For overskirt, follow **Transferring Patterns**, page 80, and refer to **Fig. 1** to transfer design to lower left corner of solid-colored fabric.

2 Follow **Making Fusible Fabric Appliqués**, page 84, to make appliqués.

3 Using transferred pattern for placement, fuse all appliqués to overskirt.

4 Transfer detail lines to appliqués.

5 Refer to **Appliqué**, page 86, to zigzag stitch around appliqué edges using clear thread.

Fig. 1

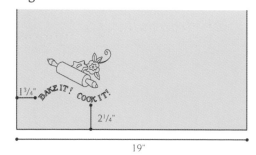

6 Follow **Embroidery Stitches**, page 81, and use 3 strands of floss to work Stem Stitches around edges of each piece, over detail lines, for outline of words, and for tendril. Work Satin Stitches inside words and for highlights on rolling pin and flower. Work French Knots on ends of handle and to secure button to center of flower.

7 Sew rickrack 1¹/₂" from lower edge of overskirt.

8 Matching right sides and short edges, fold overskirt in half. Stitch along raw edges, leaving an opening for turning. Clip corners; turn right side out and press.

9 To hem underskirt, press 1 long edge and 2 short edges of print fabric piece ¹/₄" to wrong side twice. For upper edge, press remaining long edge ¹/₄" to wrong side; press ³/₄" to wrong side. Stitch along pressed edges.

10 Center and baste upper edge of overskirt 1¹/₄" below upper edge of underskirt. To gather apron, use a wide zigzag stitch to stitch approximately 1³/₈" from top edge over heavy thread or dental floss.

11 Gather apron to approximately 15¹/₂". Center and pin ribbon over zigzag stitching. Sew ribbon to apron over gathers along each edge.

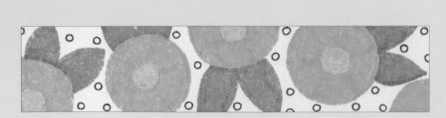

floral photo mat

To create the mat with fabric appliqués, follow these instructions. If you'd prefer to embroider or use markers, refer to the **General Instructions**, page 79, for information on transferring patterns, embroidery stitches, and using markers.

To make your project easier and more enjoyable, we encourage you to carefully read the General Instructions, page 79.

supplies
- 8" x 10" (20 cm x 25 cm) photograph **or** photocopy of photograph trimmed to 8" x 7" (20 cm x 18 cm)
- Two 12" x 6" (30 cm x 15 cm) rectangles of light-colored fabric
- Fabric scraps for appliqués
- Paper-backed fusible web
- 1 yd (91 cm) of $^3/_8$" (10 mm) wide ribbon
- Embroidery floss
- 8" x 10" (20 cm x 25 cm) photo frame
- Two 8" x 10" (20 cm x 25 cm) pieces of lightweight cardboard
- Craft glue
- Transfer supplies (see page 80)

instructions
Use pattern in envelope.

1 Follow **Transferring Patterns**, page 80, to transfer design to each fabric rectangle.

2 Follow **Making Fusible Fabric Appliqués**, page 84, to make appliqués.

3 Using transferred pattern for placement, fuse all appliqués to fabric rectangles.

4 Follow **Embroidery Stitches**, page 81, and use 3 strands of floss to work Stem Stitches around each flower, flower center, and leaves. Work French Knots in between the flowers.

5 Centering the design, trim each rectangle to 8" x 2".

6 To make mat, cut a 6³/₄" x 6¹/₈" opening in 1 cardboard piece. Glue lengths of ribbon to mat along left and right sides of opening.

7 Glue appliquéd fabric pieces to mat above and below opening. Glue lengths of ribbon to mat above and below opening.

8 Layer mat, photo, and remaining cardboard piece, gluing to hold photo in place.

9 Insert mat in frame.

all a-twitter quilt

Finished Size: 42" x 56½"
(107 cm x 144 cm)

To make your project easier and more enjoyable, we encourage you to carefully read the General Instructions, page 79.

supplies

- 3½ yds (3.2 m) **total** of assorted fabrics for quilt top
- 1⅝ yds (1.5 m) of fabric for backing
- Fabric scraps for appliqués
- Batting
- Three ⅜" (10 mm) diameter black buttons
- Paper-backed fusible web
- Embroidery floss
- Clear monofilament thread
- Stabilizer

Fig. 1

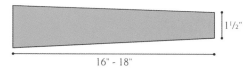

instructions

Use pattern in envelope. Match right sides and raw edges and use a ¼" seam allowance unless otherwise stated.

1 For the quilt top, cut strips 16"–18" long from assorted fabrics, making each strip narrower on one end, but at least 1½" wide (**Fig. 1**). You will need approximately 75-85 strips.

2 Matching long edges and alternating the wide and narrow ends, sew enough strips together to make a panel that is at least 58" long (approximately 25-28 strips). Press all seam allowances in one direction. Make three panels. Trim each panel to 15" wide.

3 Matching long edges and adjusting the placement of the panels so that no two like fabrics are together, sew the three panels together to make the quilt top. Trim the quilt top to 43" x 57½".

4 Follow **Making Fusible Fabric Appliqués**, page 84, to make appliqués.

5 Fuse all appliqués to quilt top.

6 Refer to **Appliqué**, page 86, to zigzag stitch around appliqué edges using clear thread.

7 Follow **Embroidery Stitches**, page 81, and use 6 strands of floss to work Blanket Stitches around edges of bird and inner wing. Work Stem Stitches around outer wing and eye. Work Stem Stitches and French Knots for birds' crown.

8 Sew buttons to birds for eyes.

9 Cut one rectangle each from backing fabric and batting the same size as the quilt top. Layer the quilt top and backing, right sides together; place the batting on top.

10 Leaving an opening for turning and using a $1/2$" seam allowance, sew the top, backing, and batting together; trim the corners. Turn the quilt right side out; press. Hand sew the opening closed.

11 Work Feather Stitches along each seamline. As you stitch, go through all layers about every 8"-10" to secure batting.

cute cushions!

mushroom pin cushion

supplies

- Red, gold, and white wool felt
- Lightweight cardboard
- Polyester fiberfill
- Fabric glue
- Pinking shears
- Small plastic bag of fine sand

instructions

Use patterns in envelope.

1 From red felt, cut 2 tops. From gold felt, cut 2 bottoms. From white felt, cut 1 base, 2 stems, and 12 dots. Using outer grey line on bottom pattern, cut shape from cardboard.

2 For mushroom cap, use a $1/4$" seam allowance to sew tops together. Glue dots to top; allow to dry. Follow **Embroidery Stitches**, page 81, and use 3 strands of floss to work Blanket Stitches around dots.

3 Center and glue cardboard shape to 1 felt bottom. Fold edges to opposite side and glue to cardboard.

4 Fold edge of top about $1/8$" to wrong side. Leaving an opening for stuffing, hand sew edge of underside to folded edge of top. Firmly stuff and sew closed.

5 Place stem pieces together. Use 2 strands of floss to work Blanket Stitches along side edges, joining pieces. Pin base to stem. Work Blanket Stitches to attach base to stem.

6 Insert sand bag into the stem. Firmly stuff remainder of stem with fiberfill. Glue tabs on top of stem to bottom.

7 Using inner grey line on bottom pattern and pinking shears, cut a hole in remaining felt bottom. Using pinking shears, trim approximately $3/8$" from outer edge of bottom. Cut through bottom and place bottom around stem. Glue bottom around stem to cover tabs.

Instructions for Owl on page 68.

owl pin cushion

supplies

- Brown, beige, gold, and white wool felt
- Polyester fiberfill
- Two $1/8$" (3 mm) black buttons
- Small plastic bag of fine sand
- Fabric glue

instructions

Use patterns in envelope.

1 From brown felt, cut 2 head back/ front pieces, 2 wings and 1 head sides. From beige felt, cut 2 body back/front pieces and 1 body sides. From gold felt, cut 2 feet and 1 beak. From white felt, cut eye mask.

2 Stack feet together. Follow **Embroidery Stitches**, page 81, and use 2 strands of floss to work Straight Stitches on scalloped edge for claws. Work Running Stitches to sew remaining edges together.

3 For body, pin body front to body sides with narrow end of sides overlapping at top. Work Blanket Stitches to attach body front to body sides. Repeat for body back, placing bag of sand in body and firmly stuffing remainder of body with fiberfill.

4 Fold each wing in half along dashed line. Work Blanket Stitches around raw edges.

5 For head, glue beak to head front. Work Blanket Stitches around eye mask. Work Stem Stitch around beak. Sew buttons to eye mask.

6 Pin head front to head sides. Work Blanket Stitches to attach head front to head sides. Pin head sides to head back. Work Blanket Stitches to attach head sides to head back. Firmly stuff head with fiberfill and work Blanket Stitches to attach head front and head back together.

7 Glue body to feet, wings to body, and head to body.

bag it! tag it!

supplies

- 12" x 16" (30 cm x 41 cm) piece of print fabric
- Blue and green felt scraps
- Embroidery floss
- Polyester fiberfill
- 7/8" (22 mm) diameter button
- 14" (36 cm) of 3/8" (10 mm) wide velvet ribbon

instructions

Use patterns in envelope. Match right sides and raw edges and use a 1/4" seam allowance.

1 Matching long edges, fold fabric rectangle in half. Leaving an opening for turning, sew edges together. Turn right side out and press. Turn rectangle inside itself to form a "self-lining."

2 Using patterns, cut 2 flowers from blue felt and 2 leaves from green felt.

3 Follow **Embroidery Stitches**, page 81, and use 2 strands of floss to work Stem Stitches for veins in leaves. Sew button to 1 flower.

4 Layer flowers with leaves and ribbon sandwiched in between; pin. Work Blanket Stitches around edge of flowers, catching leaves and ribbon in stitching. Tie a knot at end of ribbon.

5 Place gift in bag and tie with ribbon to close.

from me to you

clever notions keeper

supplies

- $8^1/_2$" x $7^3/_4$" (22 cm x 20 cm) piece **each** of black wool felt and red print fabric
- Brown, red, and green wool felt scraps
- Yellow print fabric scrap
- Embroidery floss
- $8^1/_2$" (22 cm) piece of green jumbo rickrack
- Polyester fiberfill
- Two $^3/_8$" (10 mm) diameter brown buttons
- Clear monofilament thread
- Pinking shears
- Fabric glue

instructions

Use patterns in envelope.

1 Use patterns to cut stem from brown felt, cherry from red felt, and 2 leaves from green felt. Using grey line on pattern, cut a small slit in cherry.

2 For lining, press each edge of print fabric $^1/_4$" to wrong side. Center lining on black felt. Zigzag stitch lining to felt using clear thread.

3 Follow **Embroidery Stitches**, page 81, and work Blanket Stitches around edges of lining, being careful not to stitch through felt.

4 Sew rickrack along 1 long edge of felt. Fold this edge up 2¾". To form pockets, refer to **Fig. 1** to machine stitch dividers.

5 Refer to **Fig. 2** and use 3 strands of floss and a Running Stitch to sew cherry and stem to outside of notions keeper. Insert a small bit of fiberfill under cherry before working final stitches. Sew buttons to sewing kit.

6 Using pinking shears, trim yellow fabric to 2" x 1¾". Position rectangle on top right corner of lining. Being careful not to stitch through felt, use floss and a Running stitch to sew rectangle to lining along top edge.

7 Glue a 4½" length of brown floss to end of 1 leaf; allow to dry. Stack leaves with a small amount of fiberfill between them. Work Running Stitches to join leaves. Tie floss to button on end opposite cherry.

Fig. 1

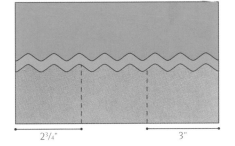

2¾"   3"

Fig. 2

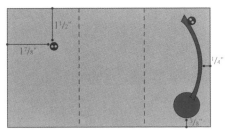

1½"

1⅞"

¼"

⅜"

for twice as nice gifts

tag #1

Finished Size: 4¹/₂" x 2³/₄" (11 cm x 7 cm)

*To make your project easier and more enjoyable, we encourage you to carefully read the **General Instructions**, page 79. Supplies and instructions are for making 1 tag.*

supplies
- 2³/₄" x 5¹/₂" (7 cm x 14 cm) piece of pink felt
- Two 4" x 4" (10 cm x 10 cm) pieces of white felt
- 2" (5 cm) tall chipboard letter
- Assorted ribbon and rickrack
- Prismacolor® Premier markers or permanent fabric markers
- Embroidery floss
- Fabric glue
- Liquid fray preventative
- Pinking shears
- Transfer supplies (see page 80)

instructions
Use pattern in envelope.

1 To make tag, fold 1 short edge of pink felt over 1". Follow **Embroidery Stitches**, page 81, and use 3 strands of floss to secure folded edge with Running Stitches along cut edge. Cut a ¹/₂" wide slit at the top center edge near fold. Trim remaining short edge with pinking shears.

2 Follow **Transferring Patterns**, page 80, to transfer flower to 1 piece of white felt.

3 Work Stem Stitches along all design lines.

4 Follow **Using Markers**, page 83, to color design.

5 Glue colored felt piece to remaining felt piece; allow to dry. Cut out flower just outside design.

6 Glue rickrack to tag; trim ends even with tag; apply fray preventative. Glue flower and letter to tag. Insert ribbons through slit at top of tag.

1

2

3

tag #2

Finished Size: 5³/₄" x 3" (15 cm x 8 cm)

*To make your project easier and more enjoyable, we encourage you to carefully read the **General Instructions**, page 79. Supplies and instructions are for making 1 tag.*

supplies

- Two 5³/₄" x 3" (15 cm x 8 cm) pieces of print fabric
- 6" x 6" (15 cm x 15 cm) piece of light-colored fabric
- 6" x 6" (15 cm x 15 cm) piece of heavyweight fusible interfacing
- Assorted ribbons, rickrack, and twill tape
- Embroidery floss
- Liquid fray preventative
- Scalloped-edge scissors
- Transfer supplies (see page 80)

instructions

Use pattern in envelope.

1 Refer to **Fig. 1** to trim corners on 1 short end of each print rectangle.

2 For tag, match wrong sides and raw edges and sew tag together ¹/₈" from edges. Using scalloped-edge scissors, trim remaining short edge of tag.

3 Follow **Transferring Patterns**, page 80, to transfer design to center of light-colored fabric.

4 Follow **Embroidery Stitches**, page 81, and use 3 strands of floss to work Satin Stitches for flowers and leaves and Stem Stitches around flowers.

5 Fuse interfacing to wrong side of fabric.

6 With design in 1 corner, trim fabric to 2³/₈" x 4¹/₄". Stitch rectangle on tag using 2 curvy lines of stitching over edge.

7 Zigzag stitch ribbon and twill tape along end of tag. Trim ends even with edges of tag. Apply fray preventative to ends of ribbons.

8 Cut a small slit at top of tag. Loop assorted ribbons and rickrack through tag.

Fig. 1

¹/₂"
⁵/₈"

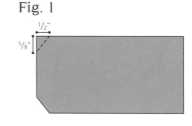

tag #3

Finished Size: 5¹/₂" x 3¹/₂" (14 cm x 9 cm)

supplies

- Light pink, dark pink, and green felt scraps
- 2¹/₂" x 4¹/₂" (6 cm x 11 cm) piece of print fabric
- Assorted ribbons
- Embroidery floss
- Scalloped-edge scissors
- Fabric glue
- ¹/₄" (6 mm) hole punch

instructions

Use pattern in envelope.

1 For tag, use scalloped-edge scissors to cut a 5¹/₂" x 3¹/₂" rectangle of dark pink felt.

2 Center and glue fabric rectangle to tag around edges. Glue ribbon lengths around edges of rectangle.

3 Use patterns to cut 4 flowers and 4 leaf clusters from felt.

4 Follow **Embroidery Stitches**, page 81, and use 3 strands of floss to work Satin Stitches for flower centers and Stem Stitches for petal details. Work Straight Stitches for the vein in the leaves. Glue leaves and flowers to tag.

5 Punch a hole on 1 end of tag. Loop assorted ribbons through tag.

glamour to go

To create the jewelry roll with embroidery, follow these instructions. If you'd prefer to make fabric appliqués or use markers, refer to the **General Instructions**, page 79, for information on transferring patterns, making fabric appliqués, and embroidery stitches.

To make your project easier and more enjoyable, we encourage you to carefully read the General Instructions, page 79.

supplies
- ³⁄₈ yd (34 cm) of solid-color fabric
- 9" x 11" (23 cm x 28 cm) piece of print fabric #1
- 6" x 12" (15 cm x 30 cm) piece of print fabric #2
- Embroidery floss
- 1¹⁄₂ yds (1.4 m) of 1" (25 mm) wide grosgrain ribbon
- 9" (23 cm) zipper
- Polyester fiberfill
- Snap
- Transfer supplies (see page 80)

instructions
Use pattern in envelope. Match right sides and raw edges and use a ¹⁄₄" seam allowance throughout.

1 From solid-color fabric, cut outer rectangle 19¹⁄₂" x 10¹⁄₂" and lining 17¹⁄₂" x 10¹⁄₂".

2 From print fabric #1, cut one pocket 10¹⁄₂" x 6³⁄₄" and two tabs 1¹⁄₂" x 1¹⁄₂".

3 From print fabric #2, cut rectangle 2¹⁄₂" x 10¹⁄₂" and ring holder 2¹⁄₂" x 9¹⁄₄".

4 Follow **Transferring Patterns**, page 80, and refer to **Fig. 1** to transfer design to outer rectangle.

5 Follow **Embroidery Stitches**, page 81, and use 3 strands of floss to work Satin Stitches for flowers, flower centers, and leaves. Work Stem Stitches and French Knots for tendrils.

6 Press 1 long raw edge of pocket ¹⁄₂" to **right** side. Overlap 1 zipper tape over folded edge; topstitch in place.

Fig. 1

7 Press remaining long raw edge of pocket ¼" to **wrong** side. Refer to **Fig. 2** (page 78) to position pocket on lining. Topstitch pressed edge of pocket and remaining side of zipper tape to lining.

8 Press 3 edges of each tab ¼" to wrong side. Place pressed edge opposite raw edge of tab over each end of zipper tape just outside zipper stop; topstitch in place. Repeat with remaining tab. Trim ends of tabs even with edge of lining.

Instructions continued on page 78.

9 For necklace/bracelet loops, cut five 2½" lengths of ribbon. Fold each length in half. Pin ribbon lengths to lining approximately 1" apart. Baste ribbon ends to lining ¼" from edge. Sew 2½" x 10½" rectangle of print fabric #2 to lining with loops sandwiched in between.

10 Fold ring holder in half lengthwise. Sew along long edge and 1 short edge. Turn right side out. Stuff ring holder with fiberfill. Press raw edges ¼" to wrong side. Machine Satin Stitch along this end, closing ring holder. Use machine Satin Stitches to attach remaining end to lining.

11 Sew snap to loose end of ring holder and to lining.

12 Fold remaining ribbon length in half. On end with embroidery, pin fold of ribbon to right side of outer rectangle at center of short edge.

13 Leaving an opening for turning, sew lining to outer rectangle with ribbon sandwiched in between. Turn right side out and press. Sew opening closed.

Fig. 2

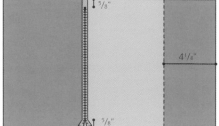

general instructions

pre-washing

First, a little preparation — we recommend that fabrics be washed, dried, and pressed. Also, garments and other purchased items, such as towels and pillowcases, that will be worn or used and laundered later should be washed, dried, and pressed before making projects. Do not use fabric softener or dryer sheets.

creating your project

There are 3 ways to create your one-of-a-kind project. The lines of the pattern can simply be embroidered. To add more color, the lines and details of the pattern can be embroidered and then the areas within the embroidery can be filled using markers. If you're up for a little more of a challenge, a fabric appliqué can be made for each area of the design and the details can be added using embroidery stitches. Instructions for each of these techniques are given on pages 81-85.

Regardless of the method you choose, you will need to transfer the pattern to the background fabric, garment, towel, canvas, etc.

transferring patterns

Before transferring, look at the pattern(s)—based on your chosen technique, decide which details of the pattern you want to transfer; you may choose less details. Trace and transfer only the desired lines.

for embroidery or fusible fabric appliqués
• water-soluble fabric pen
• tracing paper (optional)

If the fabric is light-colored and/or lightweight enough, place the pattern under the fabric and trace the desired lines of the pattern with a water-soluble pen. If you can't quite see through the fabric, trace the pattern onto tracing paper and tape it and the fabric to a sunny window; then, trace the pattern onto the fabric.

After your project is completed, remove any visible marks with a damp cotton swab.

for markers
• #2 pencil
• tracing paper (optional)
• fabric eraser (optional)

If the fabric is light-colored and/or lightweight enough, place the pattern under the fabric and trace the desired lines of the pattern **very lightly** with a #2 pencil; trace just heavy enough to barely be seen. If you can't quite see through the fabric, trace the pattern onto tracing paper and tape it and the fabric to a sunny window; then, trace the pattern onto the fabric.

3 methods

Now let's look at the 3 methods for making spectacular projects for baby, home, or to give as gifts.

embroidery stitches

You may choose to embroider the design. Choose from the stitches shown and use the number of floss strands indicated in the project instructions.

Backstitch

Backstitch is great for detail lines or outlining.

Come up at 1, go down at 2, and come up at 3 (**Fig. 1**). The length of stitches may be varied as desired.

Blanket Stitch

Blanket Stitch is often used to finish the edges of appliqués.

Come up at 1. Go down at 2 and come up at 3, keeping floss below point of needle (**Fig. 2**). Continue working as shown in **Fig. 3**.

Chain Stitch

Chain Stitch works well for thicker, more prominent detail lines.

Come up at 1 and go down again at 1 to form a loop (**Fig. 4**). Keeping loop below point of needle, come up at 2 and go down again at 2 to form second loop. Continue making loops or "chain" until desired length is reached. Make a small straight stitch over the last loop (**Fig. 5**).

Fig. 1
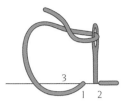

Fig. 2
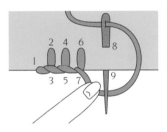

Fig. 3
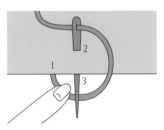

Fig. 4

Fig. 5

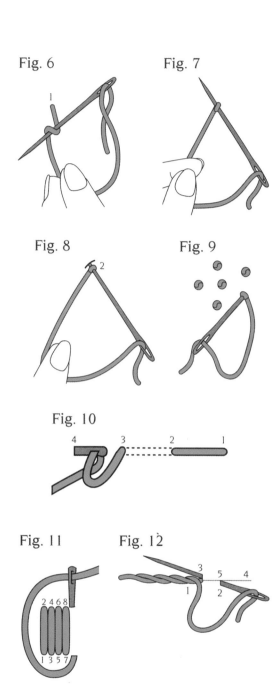

Fig. 6   Fig. 7

Fig. 8   Fig. 9

Fig. 10

French Knot

French Knots are commonly used for eyes, highlights, or other accents.

Follow **Figs. 6 – 9** to complete each French Knot. Come up at 1. Wrap floss once around needle and insert needle at 2, holding end of floss with non-stitching fingers. Tighten knot, then pull needle through, holding floss until it must be released.

Running Stitch

Running Stitch is great to use for basting two pieces of fabric together or for a broken detail line.

The Running Stitch consists of a series of Straight Stitches with the stitch length equal to the space between stitches. Come up at 1, go down at 2, and come up at 3 (**Fig. 10**).

Satin Stitch

Satin Stitch is typically used to fill an area such as a flower center.

Referring to **Fig. 11** and keeping stitches touching but not overlapping, come up at 1, go down at 2, and come up at 3. Go down at 4, come up at 5, and go down at 6.

Fig. 11   Fig. 12

Stem Stitch

Stem Stitch can be used to outline a design and to add detail lines.

Referring to **Fig. 12**, come up at 1. Keeping the floss below the stitching line, go down at 2 and come up at 3. Go down at 4 and come up at 5.

Straight Stitch

Straight Stitches are used where straight lines are needed such as the duck's feathers, page 12.

Fig. 13

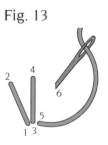

Come up at 1 and go down at 2 (**Fig. 13**). Length of stitches may be varied as desired.

using markers

Did you love coloring with markers when you were a kid? This technique is just the same but will leave you with more sophisticated results. And adding a little stem stitching around the areas of the design makes a great finishing touch!

For our models we used Prismacolor® Premier markers. If the project will not be laundered, Prismacolor® Premier markers are a good choice for their wide variety of colors and great blendability. If the project will be laundered, be sure to use permanent fabric markers for coloring your designs. Follow manufacturer's instructions for any information about heat setting.

Test the markers on a scrap of your fabric before beginning a project to determine how much each marker will bleed. Most markers will bleed when applied to fabric. The trick is to get the bleeding to work for you. For photo A, we colored up to the drawn lines and the marker bled outside the lines. For photo B, we did not color all the way to the drawn lines and the marker stayed inside the lines. Once you've finished, you can carefully fill in spots with the markers as needed.

Just as an added precaution, even if using permanent fabric markers, launder the scrap of fabric to check color-fastness.

photo A

photo B

techniques:

- Always practice on a scrap piece of the fabric you are using for your project before coloring on your project. You will be able to see what the color looks like on that particular fabric; the colors often change as they dry. You should also test blending different colors together.
- Use the smallest tip of the marker and use very small, light brush-like strokes.
- When layering or blending colors, start with the lightest color first. Once you've put one layer of your lightest color on, let that dry. It will act like a basecoat and the top layers should not bleed as much.
- For blending, work fast…they do dry quickly. You get a better look if the ink is wet when you are blending. Laying down a color of similar or equal value next to a previously applied color before it dries will allow the marker colors to bleed into each other.

- Often the artwork has highlights in the design. For example, the small blue owl has highlights on his tummy. To get this look, simply leave the highlighted area uncolored. As you get closer to the highlight use the lightest color possible and press down very lightly, barely brushing the tip of the marker to the fabric. The closer you get to the highlight, the lighter you press.

- Here's an example of how the letters on the "Birds of a Feather" pillow were colored. We used three different colors – a yellow, a medium red, and a dark red. First, we colored all the letters with yellow, the lightest color. By the time we were finished with the last letter, the first one was dry enough to begin blending. We quickly colored one letter at a time. We started with the dark red and colored from the bottom up. Where the colors started to blend we pressed more lightly, then switched to the medium red. When we were finished with the medium red, we colored over the whole letter with the yellow marker. This really helped the colors blend well.

making fusible fabric appliqués

For added charm and interest, you may choose to include fabric appliqués for each area of the design. For the appliqués, choose medium-weight 100% cotton fabrics.

If you're making fabric appliqués for a washable project, wash and dry background fabric, garment, towel, etc. and all fabrics for appliqués without using fabric softener or dryer sheets; press.

White or light-colored fabrics may need to be lined with fusible interfacing before applying fusible web to prevent darker fabrics from showing through.

To make the appliqués more durable, zigzag all raw edges of the appliqués. This is especially important if item will be worn or used and washed.

1 Transfer entire design to background fabric, garment, towel, etc.

2 For appliqué pieces, you will need to reverse the patterns. To make a reversed pattern, trace appliqué shape onto tracing paper, turn tracing paper over, and re-trace the drawn lines. Make patterns from artwork (see **Making Patterns**, below).

3 Place paper-backed fusible web, paper side up, over appliqué pattern. Trace the reversed patterns onto paper side of web with pencil as many times as indicated in project instructions for a single fabric.

4 Rough cut pieces from web approximately $1/4$" outside drawn lines. Follow manufacturer's instructions to fuse web pieces to wrong side of fabrics. Cut pieces out along outer drawn lines. (*Note: Some pieces may be given as measurements. Fuse web to wrong side of fabrics indicated for these pieces. Use rotary cutting equipment to cut out these appliqué pieces.*) Remove paper backing and fuse to background, following transferred lines for placement.

Note: If adding fusible appliqués, the steam from the iron may remove some of the drawn lines from the fabric marking pen; re-apply as needed.

making patterns

Types of Patterns
You'll need to look at the design and decide which pieces are layered and which overlap one another. The techniques for making patterns for the different situations vary just a bit.

For pieces that are layered, no underlap is necessary. A pattern will be needed for the base and for each separate appliqué that will be layered on the base. A good example of this is the Owls, page 10. You need a body pattern for the base and separate patterns for the tummy, eye mask, feet, etc. (**Fig. 14**).

For pieces that overlap, you will need to add a $1/8$" to $1/4$" underlap to the underneath piece. A good example of this is the Flower Bib, page 26. The leaves are cut $1/8$" to $1/4$" larger as shown (**Fig. 15**).

Fig. 14

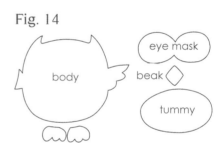

Fig. 15

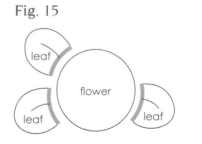

Cutting Patterns
For patterns for pieces without underlaps, place tracing paper over the reversed design. Trace each portion of the design separately. Cut out traced patterns.

To make patterns for overlapped pieces, place tracing paper over the reversed design. Trace each portion of the design separately, adding underlaps as necessary. Cut out traced patterns.

Fig. 16

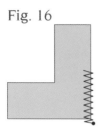

Fig. 17

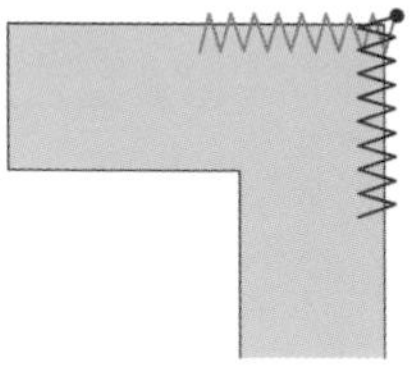

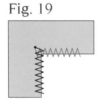

Fig. 18

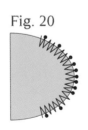

Fig. 19

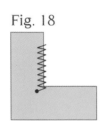

Fig. 20

Fig. 21

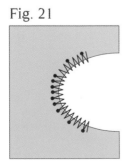

appliqué

To make your appliqués more durable for laundering, zigzag all raw edges of the appliqués using clear monofilament thread in the machine needle and general all-purpose thread that matches the background fabric in the bobbin.

1 Pin stabilizer, such as paper or any of the commercially available products, on wrong side of background fabric before stitching appliqués in place.

2 Set sewing machine for a medium (approximately ¹/₈") zigzag stitch and a medium stitch length. Slightly loosening the top tension may yield a smoother stitch.

3 Begin by stitching two or three stitches in place (drop feed dogs or set stitch length at 0) to anchor thread. Most of the zigzag stitch should be on the appliqué with the right edge of the stitch falling at the outside edge of the appliqué. Stitch over all exposed raw edges of appliqué pieces.

4 (**Note**: Dots on **Figs. 16 – 21** indicate where to leave needle in fabric when pivoting.) For outside corners, stitch just past corner, stopping with needle in background fabric (**Fig. 16**). Raise presser foot. Pivot project, lower presser foot, and stitch adjacent side (**Fig. 17**).

5 For inside corners, stitch just past corner, stopping with needle in appliqué fabric (**Fig. 18**). Raise presser foot. Pivot project, lower presser foot, and stitch adjacent side (**Fig. 19**).

6 When stitching outside curves, stop with needle in background fabric. Raise presser foot and pivot project as needed. Lower presser foot and continue stitching, pivoting as often as necessary to follow curve (**Fig. 20**).

7 When stitching inside curves, stop with needle in appliqué fabric. Raise presser foot and pivot project as needed. Lower presser foot and continue stitching, pivoting as often as necessary to follow curve (**Fig. 21**).

8 Do not backstitch at end of stitching. Pull threads to wrong side of background fabric; knot thread and trim ends.

9 Carefully tear away stabilizer.

adding welting

1 To make welting, measure edges of pillow top and add 4". Measure circumference of cord and add 2". Cut a bias strip of fabric the determined measurements, piecing if necessary.

2 Lay cord along center of bias strip on wrong side of fabric; fold strip over cord. Using a zipper foot, machine baste along length of strip close to cord. Trim seam allowance to the width you will use to sew pillow top and back together (see project).

3 Matching raw edges and beginning and ending 3" from ends of welting, baste welting to right side of pillow top. To make turning corners easier, clip seam allowance of welting at pillow top corners.

4 Remove approximately 3" of seam at 1 end of welting; fold fabric away from cord. Trim remaining end of welting so that cord ends meet exactly (**Fig. 22**).

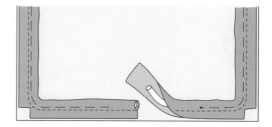

Fig. 22

5 Fold short edge of welting fabric ½" to wrong side; fold fabric back over area where ends meet (**Fig. 23**).

6 Baste remainder of welting to pillow top close to cord (**Fig. 24**).

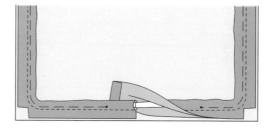

Fig. 23

7 Place pillow back and pillow top right sides together. Sew pillow top and back together, leaving an opening at bottom edge for turning.

8 Turn pillow right side out, carefully pushing corners outward. Stuff with polyester fiberfill or pillow form and sew final closure by hand.

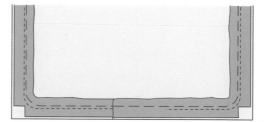

Fig. 24

Special thanks to Nelwyn Gray, Kelly Reider, and
Linda Tiano for project finishing and model testing.

We want to extend a warm thank you to the DMC Corporation
for the embroidery floss used in this book.

Metric Conversion Chart	
Inches x 2.54 = centimeters (cm)	Yards x .9144 = meters (m)
Inches x 25.4 = millimeters (mm)	Yards x 91.44 = centimeters (cm)
Inches x .0254 = meters (m)	Centimeters x .3937 = inches (")
	Meters x 1.0936 = yards (yd)

Standard Equivalents					
1/8"	3.2 mm	0.32 cm	1/8 yard	11.43 cm	0.11 m
1/4"	6.35 mm	0.635 cm	1/4 yard	22.86 cm	0.23 m
3/8"	9.5 mm	0.95 cm	3/8 yard	34.29 cm	0.34 m
1/2"	12.7 mm	1.27 cm	1/2 yard	45.72 cm	0.46 m
5/8"	15.9 mm	1.59 cm	5/8 yard	57.15 cm	0.57 m
3/4"	19.1 mm	1.91 cm	3/4 yard	68.58 cm	0.69 m
7/8"	22.2 mm	2.22 cm	7/8 yard	80 cm	0.8 m
1"	25.4 mm	2.54 cm	1 yard	91.44 cm	0.91 m